WHY 2K iS OK!™

BY JON AND PAUL KENDALL

CONTRIBUTING EDITOR: WARREN ARBOGAST

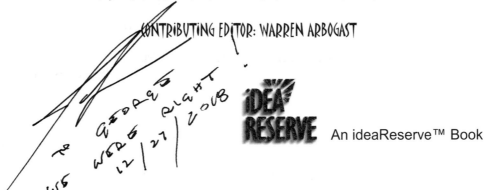

TO GEORGE
WE WERE RIGHT!
12/27/2008

iDEA RESERVE

An ideaReserve™ Book

An ideaReserve™ Book
www.ideareserve.com

1st edition, July 1999

Printed in the United States of America

Library of Congress Cataloging-in-Publication Data is available.
ISBN-0-9644648-9-6

1 3 5 7 9 10 8 6 4 2

Table of Contents

Introduction

When Jon and Paul Kendall asked me to write the introduction for WHY 2K IS OK!, I was concerned that making light of a serious problem was not appropriate for a Member of Congress. Then I thought about it more and more, and decided that humor may be one way to help us through a potentially trying time!

WHY 2K IS OK! is a humorous look at the Y2K problem from a lighthearted perspective. Make no mistake: this could be a serious problem for us all, but raising awareness of what we will need to do to prepare for Y2K is the ultimate purpose of this book. The "Resources" section provides a number of great links to World Wide Web sites, books, and articles that will help you and your family understand the scope of the problem, and make preparations. Then pick up WHY 2K IS OK! and enjoy!

Representative Connie Morella, 8th District, Maryland
Chair, House Committee on Science, Co-Chair, House Year 2000 Task Force,
www.house.gov/morella/sci&tech.htm

The Millennium Bug

The Year 2000 computer problem, dubbed the "Y2K or Millennium Bug," relates to the process that many computers and "embedded" microchips use to record and manipulate calendar dates. Typically, computers and many people express the date in a six-digit date field, for example 12/10/62. The use of only two numerals to express the year is at the heart of the problem for computers.

> "Leave it to the computer industry
> to shorten the name of the Year 2000
> problem to Y2K. That's what got us into
> this problem in the first place!"
>
> — Anonymous Web wisdom

We expect that computer and related systems will have a hard time at Y2K because they can't determine whether 01/01/00 refers to January 1, 2000 or to 1900. If your Millenium New Year's Party is going well, you might have the same problem…

At the stroke of midnight heralding in January 1, 2000, experts, politicians, bureaucrats, kooks, and John Q. Public believe computers controlling everything from airplanes to milking machines to power grids to microwave ovens will fail. Yup, they won't be working, kaput! The computers will think it's 1900, and so will you.

Think about it! Computers will believe they're in 1900…
- William (Bill) McKinley is President.
- The nation is on an environmental upswing, and hiking and mountaineering are all the rage.
- Terrorism is getting out of control. The President is a target, and there are assassinations around the world.

- Women are entering the workforce in increasing numbers.
- New inventions and the fast pace of technology overwhelm the nation: motion pictures, automobiles, phonographs, electric lights, and indoor plumbing.
- Public debates about moral character are raging.
- The music business is booming.
- Environmentally-friendly electric cars (streetcars that is!) are coming on-line.
- Predictions are about new technologies making life better for the World.
- Times are good.

And what's so different from today?   Maybe the computers have the right idea…

- Progress was on everyone's mind.
- New inventions and small businesses were popping up.
- The economy was booming.
- Cynicism and self-pity were OUT.
- The Declaration of Independence was IN.
- And those citizens "without" worked hard to get "within!"

Or, maybe all hell will break loose...

- Telephone calls will be cut off or you'll be billed for 99 years of talk time.
- ATM machines won't give you your money, or will give you too much money.
- Coffee machines will not brew. (This could be real trouble at Starbucks.)

- Cars won't start.
- Electric blankets chill.
- Hot tubs stop bubbling.
- Weapons systems won't function. (A moment of computer-induced peace!)
- Security systems won't let you into or out of work. (Wow, what a shame!)
- Utility company computers will shut down water, electricity and gas.
- School districts will summon all 105 year olds to Kindergarten.
  (This already happened!)

"January 1 is a Saturday. So if the world comes
to an end for a couple of days, it'll be OK.
We've all had weekends like that."

– Former FCC chair.

So Whose Fault is this Anyway?

God appears in a dream to three people: Russian President Boris Yeltsin, American President Bill Clinton and Microsoft CEO Bill Gates. To each of them, God says, "You are one of the three most powerful men on Earth. I want you to know, that it is very bad what mankind has done to Mother Earth. Therefore, before the year 2000 begins, I will cleanse the Earth with a huge flood." The next morning Boris Yeltsin in the State Duma says: "I've got lots of bad news. First, God exists. Second, He will destroy us all before the year 2000 with a huge flood." Bill Clinton at the White House says, "I've got good news and bad news. The good news is God exists. The bad news is that He will send a flood to destroy us all before the year 2000." Bill Gates says to his managers, "I've got lots of good news for you. First, I am one of the three most powerful men on this planet; and second, the millennium bug will not be a problem!"

- Russian Web Humor

Not that the Millennium Bug is Bill Gates' fault. If you want to get technical, the Millennium Bug isn't really a bug at all. A computer bug is an unintentional programming glitch caused by the unexpected interaction of codes within various software programs. The Millennium Bug was actually a conscious decision by the programmers of yesteryear!

Nice job folks…but in their defense, they never thought the software programs they were writing in the fifties, sixties, seventies, and even the eighties would still be in use today. Who knows why they didn't. In fact, many of these programs form the underlying backbone of large components of today's most sophisticated programs running a myriad of high-tech stuff around the world. And much of this "code" was programmed into an enormous quantity of "embedded chips;" those chips are in thousands, maybe millions of machines, sensors, microprocessors, controls, toys, cars, meters, fax machines, scales... you name it. So what happens when all this stuff drops dead at the dawn of the new millennium?

Nobody knows exactly, but there's much speculation that a catastrophe of epic proportions will ensue. Maybe an embedded chip in a valve on a ship in the North Sea will go haywire, causing the ship to stop pumping oil, which will cripple the drilling rig, which will overwhelm the corporate computers and stop the production of oil worldwide.

This begs the question, "Who caused the problem?"

Did the Antichrist cause the Millennium Bug? His predicted birth year of 1962 and his background makes him an unlikely candidate to have caused the Millennium Bug, largely believed to have been caused by trying to cram too much information on paper punch cards. The punch cards were developed for information processing around

1889 by Herman Hollerith to support the U.S. Census Bureau. He thought it would be a good idea to put the information on punch cards, not ledgers, so a machine could process the information more quickly and accurately. Nice job, Herman, but today's punch cards have only 960 bits of information, with 80 columns by 12 rows, and programmers were trying to economize the information on the cards so as not to use too much then-expensive space or memory. So, they economized by using only two digits for the year. That was a great idea at one time, but now, Nostradamus look out; Y2K is here and the ghost's in the machines! And make no mistake: punch cards are still being used at large companies and government agencies around the globe. Government computers and the Antichrist…maybe we need to rethink this…

Did lawyers cause the Millennium Bug? At the American Bar Association's 1998 convention, one attorney allegedly called Y2K "the bug that finally provides lawyers the opportunity to rule the world." Maybe this affords the answer; it is expected that the Millennium Bug could be the biggest litigation bonanza in history. It would take a great deal of patience, but maybe the lawyers caused this problem to rule the world in the 21st century. So picture an attorney hunched over Herman Hollerith's shoulder, whispering in his ear to use two digits for the date. Or picture a similar attorney years later, also part of the secret pact to finally take over the world, telling Bill Gates: "Use two digits for the date in MS-DOS. Nobody will mind."

This whole mess could have been avoided if we had used the same numerals that confounded us in elementary school. Yes, if computer developers had chosen to use Roman numerals rather than their more familiar Arabic cousins, the whole Millennium Bug, which might have been known as "YMM," might never have been an issue to begin with.

I, II, III, IV, V, VI, VII...

We were taught in elementary school that VIII (V=5 and I=1, so 5+1+1+1) is 8 and IX (X=10 and smaller numerals to the left of larger numerals are subtractive, so 10-1) is 9. Thus, a program designed in 1956 will carry a year of MCMLVI. The "MCM" works like the subtractive nature of "IX," it means "1900." Programmers might have made mistakes along the way in expressing years: for instance, "MCMLXXXXVI" and "MCMXCVI" could have been chosen to express the year 1996. Even so, the year 2000 would be expressed as MM – hard to mess up! Software programs would only have needed two places to represent the Year 2000 because "MM" actually takes less digits than the years immediately before (MCMXCIX) and after it (MMI). No Millennium Bug! In fact, sort of an Anti-Millennium Bug! And you thought that Roman Numerals would NEVER come in handy, didn't you?

Whose Calendar is IT?

Our everyday calendar is called the Gregorian Calendar. This calendar is based on the Julian Calendar, named after Julius Caesar and created around 50 BC. Julius wanted a uniform and accurate calendar with which to record important dates. Of course, before it was firmed up, the local bureaucrats had toyed with it to extend their time in office, which made the calendar wrong. Years into the Julian Calendar, Julius decided to bring in the consultants, in this case Sosigenes, the Alexandrian astronomer, to scrap the whole thing and start over.

The Julian Calendar became the now familiar 365-day a year plus an extra day every four years (leap year). Then the bureaucrats got it wrong again and they added the extra day every three years, not four, for years up to about 8 BC. So they had to change the calendar again to fix that.

In the following centuries, weeks and months were added. But, since the accuracy of the 2000-year-old stopwatches were not so good, 500 years later, spring started in winter and the dates were off again. To fix it, Pope Gregory XIII (Get it? The Gregorian Calendar!) cut 10 days from the calendar to get caught up again, and updated the leap year configuration. Needless to say, people didn't flock to change their calendars, and since the change was mandated by the Catholic Church, many Protestant and Orthodox countries stayed with the Julian Calendar.

It took about 200 years for Germany to change, another 200 for Russia to change. When the American Colonies changed to the Gregorian Calendar in 1752, the discrepancy was 11 days. So – you guessed it – the authorities added 11 days to the calendar on September 3, 1752... and presto! George Washington's birthday was moved from February 11, 1732 to February 22, 1732!

Taking into account the mess caused by development of the Julian and Gregorian Calendars, and that the Biblical Calendar had 360 days a year (some scholars argue that Christ was actually born on July 10, 02 BC), Year 2000 may well be behind us! Stupid computers don't even know that the Y2K problem is over, and there's nothing to worry about. Or, do we have extra time to complete repairs? It depends on which calendar you want to believe. Take a look…

The Calendar Clash

Gregorian	Saturday, 1 January 2000
Mayan	Long count = 12.19.6.15.0; tzolkin = 9 Ahau; haab = 8 Kankin
French	Décade II, Duodi de Nivôse de l'Année 208 de la Révolution
Islamic	24 Ramadan 1420
Hebrew	23 Teveth 5760
Julian	19 December 1999
ISO	Day 6 of week 52 of 1999
Persian	Dey 1378
Ethiopic	23 Takhsas 1993
Coptic	22 Kiyahk 1716
Chinese	Cycle 78, year 16 (Ji-Mao), month 11 (Wu-Yin), day 25 (Wu-Wu)
Julian day	2451545
Day of year	Day 1 of 2000; 365 days remaining in the year
Discordian	Sweetmorn, Chaos 1, Year of Our Lady of Discord 3166

An even more creative solution is the New Era Calendar. This non-secular calendar starts on 1-1-00, at year zero. The theory is to start fresh; the computers will think it's year zero anyway, so why spend all the money and time to change? Two digit dates are fine, and it gives us another two thousand years to figure out the Y2K crisis.

I never think of the future, it comes soon enough.

— *Albert Einstein*

And You Thought the Millennium Bug was a Problem!

Of course, we at Why2K must address not just the Year 2000 technology-related issues – the Millennium Bug. No, we are compelled to comment on any number of Why2K-related maladies. The worst and the scariest have to be the hell, fire and brimstone kind of stuff. The earthbound comets, the Seven Angels of the Apocalypse, and economic ruin caused by trouble of Biblical scale. We at Why2K do not have the connection that allows others to predict a future that lays waste to civilization as we know it…but most of these predictions are not clearly worded (to say the least) and are terrifying to boot. No, we can but state the facts as we know them, and use our crack staff and intensive research labs to distill the truth from these tomes.

The fabled Grand Cross of 1999 and the Grand Alignment of 2000 are rare astro-logical events relating to the alignment of the planets that, some say, will cause multiple natural disasters. Allegedly, on August 18, 1999, the first event, the Grand Cross, will place the planets in an unusual position to signal the Beasts of the Apocalypse…or something like that. And on May 5, 2000, the Grand Alignment will place the Earth, Moon, Sun, Mercury, Venus, Mars, Jupiter, and Saturn all in line across the Solar System. The remaining two planets will rest on the sidelines. To the untrained, this may not sound like any big deal. To the truly paranoid, this configuration pits the gravitational pull of these huge celestial bodies plus the Sun against our small, helpless Earth. The results, they insist, will include floods, earthquakes, the shifting of the earth's axis, and the general war and mayhem that goes with massive global destruction. And you thought the Millennium Bug would cause problems for your spreadsheet!

In his book *Prophecies: 2000*, Matthew Bunson has identified 125 pages of disastrous Prophecies of Darkness, and only 12 pages of positive Prophecies of Hope. That's a ten-to-one chance of bad news…not good odds. Of course, to put things in perspective, most of the positive prophecies happen AFTER the death and destruction of the time of Darkness, which of course, is NOW!

And it shall come to pass that whosever
gets safe out of war shall die in the
earthquake, and whosever gets safe out of the
earthquake shall be burned by the fire,
and whosever gets out of the fire shall
be destroyed by famine.

– Book of Baruch

And the Millennium Bug shall consume whoever gets out of famine.

– A Why2K Team member

Our favorite soothsayer-for-hire has to be the famous Nostradamus, the King of the Prophets (1503-1566). He really had a nose for trouble, allegedly calling Napoleon's and Hitler's rise to power. He also stated the date for the Antichrist's conquering arrival in July 1999 in New York City (JFK or LaGuardia is still in question) heralded by the eclipse of August 11, 1999. According to "seer" Jeane Dixon, the Antichrist was born on February 2, 1962. He's a Middle Eastern-born male named Armilus, Mabus, or Alus (or some

combination of these letters as in an anagram), with one eye larger than the other, hearing impaired, and walking with a limp. He's believed to be working at this very moment, crippling the world as we know it and causing death and destruction culminating in World War III. Please keep your eyes out, and call the proper authorities when you find him!

Finally, we were able to find an obscure passage from the little known prophet Billeous Gatesium (48 BC-01 AD). We can't be sure of the translation, where it was found, or the exact date of the passage (the Why2K team was celebrating a little hard the night before we discovered this). You must come to your own conclusions on this one.

"And on the dates of the multiple nothings,
the tools shall rise up to smite the wicked
and cause great grief to the followers
of the Evil Empire. I see great gold changing
hands to the legends who battle the evil
tools and their followers, and in the end so shall life go on."

– *Billeous Gateseum*

Y1K and YZERO Bugs

The Millennium Bug certainly can't be a new idea. Mustn't there have been problems associated with Y1K and YZERO? We have spared no expense in researching the other great millennium bugs, and much can be learned from these traumatic historical periods.

For example, during the YZERO debacle, how did the calendar keepers and scholars of the time deal with the switch from backwards numbering to forward numbering? The changeover from BC (before Christ) to AD (anno Domini, "in the year of our Lord," not "After Death") must have been a tumultuous event. Would the sand flow back to the top of the hourglass? Would the Sun rise in the West and set in the East so the sundials would work properly for the new millennium? How could they update all the existing hardware in time when they only had six days from December 25th to the January 1, 0000? And most perplexing to our team: what did they do during Christ's 33 years on Earth? And what did they do with 0 AD anyway…? Christ was born in 1 AD? But he wasn't dead yet. How did they know to count the years backwards anyway? Talk about a calendar problem...

The robed scholars and merchants of the day must have held the first blue ribbon commission on the YZERO Bug. The faux-merchant Jeff Bezosus no doubt stated "All writings shall be free of the YZERO Problem," and the oracle Ellison the Great may have commanded, "From this day forward, we shall make the products that will work for two thousand years."

THE YEAR ZERO PROBLEM:
A LETTER FROM 1 BC
(from the Web, translator Anonymous)

Are you still working on the YZERO problem? This change from BC to AD is giving us a lot of headaches, and we haven't much time left. I don't know how people will cope with working the wrong way around. Having been working happily downwards forever, now we have to start thinking upwards. You would think that someone would have thought of it earlier and not left it to us to sort it all out at this last minute.
I spoke to Caesar the other evening. He was livid that Julius hadn't done something about it when he was sorting out the calendar. He said he could see why Brutus turned nasty. We called in Consultus, but he simply said that continuing downwards using minus BC won't work and as usual charged a fortune for doing nothing useful. Surely, will we not have to throw out all our hardware and start again? Gatesious will make yet another fortune out of this I suppose.

The moneylenders are paranoid of course! They have been told that all usury rates will invert and they will have to pay their clients to take out loans. It's an ill wind....

As for myself, I just can't see the sand in an hourglass flowing upwards. We have heard that there are three wise men in the East who have been working on the problem, but unfortunately they won't arrive until it's all over. I have heard that there are plans to stable all horses at midnight at the turn of the year as there are fears that they will stop and try to run backwards, causing immense damage to chariots and possible loss of life.

Some say the world will cease to exist at the moment of transition. Anyway, we are still continuing to work on this blasted YZERO problem. I will send a tablet to you if anything further develops. If you have any ideas please let me know.

Sincerely,
Calendreceus

And for the Y1K anniversary, there was equal fear and loathing. The end of the world was near as the Bible had foretold. Or as the French cleric Raoul Glaber (no fooling) stated, "Satan will soon be unleashed because the thousand years have been completed." No food, no light, no water, the people and systems of the day would be banished to hell. Would the water clock keep time? Would the astrolabe still track the stars?

As headlined in the January 1, 1000, Special Millennium Edition of the Wall Street Journal, published (republished?) January 11, 1999, "No Apocalypse Now: Y1K Anxiety Ends, But World Doesn't; Citing Invasions and Plagues, Some Sages Warned This Is A Brief Reprieve - Till 1033. (In the end, it wasn't the end.)"

Doomsday Dates to Remember

Of course, the best way to predict the future is to review the past and see the way to the future. While working on that COBOL program trying to fix our Millennium Bug, here are a few other doomsday dates to ponder:

666   Original doomsday seen as the arrival date of the Antichrist signified by the number: 666.

1000   Obvious doomsday with the new millennium.

1033   Crucifixion of Christ plus a millennium.

1666   Year 666 plus a millennium.

1843   William Miller, the 19th-century Seventh Day Adventist, predicts the end of the world (first try).

1844   If at first you don't succeed…William Miller picks a new date.

1950   Haley's Comet.

1962	Birth of the Antichrist.
1999	Coming of the Antichrist, Grand Cross of planets.
8-22-99	Global Positioning System internal clock resets, stranding old ships, trucks and solders.
9-9-99	Great "Nines Problem" Computer Hiccup of '99 (oops, we mean 1999), 9999 means "die" in computereze.
10-1-99	Federal Government starts Fiscal Year 2000.
1-0-00	Some computers think this is the day before the BIG Day.
1-1-00	The BIG Day, planes fall out of the sky, clocks stop, electricity stops, water stops, and the Why2K-compliant equipment and services listed in this book reign supreme! (Oh, that's January 1, 2000, not 1900.)*
1-3-00	First Monday of Y2K.
3-21-00	End of the Piscine (Pisces) Age, beginning of the Age of Aquarius.
5-5-00	Planets line up in Grand Alignment.

2000	Much speculation on end of the World as we know it: economic down fall, depression, no fuel, no food, no money, no coffee, no pizza, and the Evil Empire rules the land!
01-01-01	The REAL start of the New Millennium.
2001	Edgar Cayce, the Sleeping Prophet, predicts earthquakes: New York, San Francisco (Silicon Valley?), and LA are all underwater; Nevada landowners wind up with beachfront property.
2012	The Mayan Calendar predicts the end.
2013	The Inca Calendar predicts the end.
2033	Crucifixion of Christ plus two millennia.
2666	The Antichrist tries again…666 plus two millennia.
3797	Nostradamus predicts our Sun goes Supernova. (At least we should be over the Y2K Millennium Bug by then.)

*Why2K Tip of the Day: The Federal Aviation Administration's (FAA) air traffic control systems will go Y2K at midnight Greenwich Mean Time on December 31, 1999. That's 6 PM in New York and 3 PM in Los Angeles. Keep an eye out…

Man, it's going to be a tough millennium at this rate! Stock up on food, water, and generators.

The Why2K Gallery

We are all going to need a new way of thinking and a new way of life once the Millennium Bug hits.

On the following pages, we have assembled an exhaustive collection of certified post-millennium stuff, and in many cases we compare these "OK" items with questionable Year 2000 compliant hardware, software, and services. With our vast research lab and teams of trained engineers and technicians, we have certified all the Why2k-products as being totally "Why2k-OK compliant." Hey, they worked in the last millennium, why not the new one? They need no power grid, no code; they're self sustaining, backbreaking, pain-in-the-ass, and hard-labor intensive...well, you get the idea...

Legal note: Please be advised that Why2K-certifying these devices, systems, and services, means nothing. The users of these devices, systems and services must complete the appropriate due diligence before applying the listed devices, systems and services in a post-Y2K world. You're on your own! Have a nice day.

Send your Why 2K is OK! ideas to us at:

ideas@Why2KisOK.com

The Internet

The Internet has brought a whole new world to many of us — with a whole new vocabulary. After Y2K, you'll have to relearn everything you know — and here are some Why 2K is OK answers to questions you haven't thought of yet...

www.Why2KisOK.com

THE INTERNET BACKBONE

Y2K Compliant?

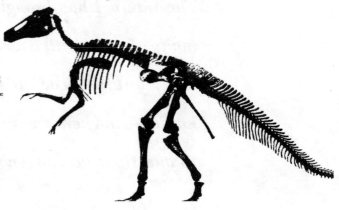

Key
- OC12c Link
- OC3c Link
- DS3 Link
- ◉ Major Internet Exchange Point
- ○ Metropolitan Service Area

Note: Map is not to scale.

1- BOSTON
2- PROVIDENCE
3- HARTFORD
4- NEWYORK
5- NEWYORK N&F
6- PHILADELPHIA/
WILMINGTON
7- BALTIMORE
8- WASHINGTON DC
9- RESS-EAST
10- ROCHESTER
11- SYRACUSE

This backbone is the architecture
guaranteed to lock up on 01/01/00...

Why 2K Certified!

...this backbone's been
solid for 60 million years!

COOKIES

Y2K Compliant?

```
Cookie File
tscape.com/newsref/std/cookie_spec.html
erated file! Do not edit

  TRUE    /       FALSE   1293832219967   UIDC     206.26.13977.6
om        FALSE   /       FALSE  9242189128        NGUserI7777777
  TRUE    /       FALSE   1082394578112   JEB2     D756777A663DC7
  TRUE    /       FALSE   946684740       12NSPOP  Imy77n5
t         TRUE    /       FALSE   192110499155     id        4449b1
om        TRUE    /       FALSE   118112140358     PreferencesID
  TRUE    /       FALSE   129379673117    SB_ID    09251422252346
  TRUE    /       FALSE   9466847113      RMID     ce1a8b42373b25
  TRUE    /       FALSE   12713611513     B        496buskkkhrtip
com       TRUE    /       FALSE  9412191913        SAFE_COOKIE
  TRUE    /       FALSE   12419135108     AA002    00926624558-34
  FALSE   /       FALSE   12937511742     EGSOFT_ID         28802.
com       FALSE   /       FALSE  1893455903        EW3_ID  206.21
```

Just what are "cookies" anyway?

Why 2K Certified!

...it really won't matter after Why 2K — as
long as you have a cow!

DOWNLOADING

Y2K Compliant?

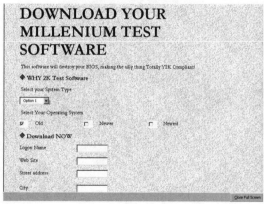

DOWNLOAD YOUR
MILLENIUM TEST
SOFTWARE

This software will destroy your BIOS, making the silly thing Totally Y2K Compliant!

◆ WHY 2K Test Software

Select your System Type

Option 1 ▾

Select Your Operating System

☑ Old ☐ Newer ☐ Newest

◆ Download NOW

Logon Name

Web Site

Street address

City

Close Full Screen

Why 2K Certified!

Downloading and storing software
used to be a click away...

...now you'll really need massive storage!

SEARCH ENGINE

Y2K Compliant?

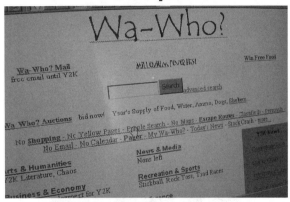

Searching cyberspace used to be a simple
thing — until your engine quits...

Why 2K Certified!

...this engine won't quit at midnight...in fact,
it's hard to stop once you get it going!

FIREWALL

Y2K Compliant?

Network engineers love to brag about
their firewalls...

Why 2K Certified!

...hackers - try penetrating this one!

FLAMING

Y2K Compliant?

WHY 2K FORUM

Your an Idiot!!!! - Dweebs 13:29:23 6/03/99 (0)
  No, You are - Mike the Bike 11:25:33 6/03/99 (2)
    Re: Pack Sand, Y2K is great- Annonimouse13:48:52 6/03/99 (0)
      Re: - No, You are - Haggar 11:41:50 6/03/99 (0)

This book stinks-- Les Johnson 08:18:24 6/03/99 (0)
  NO IT DON"T -- Luap Lladnek 21:43:19 6/02/99 (3)
    YUP IT DO - Haggar 05:33:31 6/03/99 (2)
      SEZ WHO- Mudwolf 09:40:44 6/03/99 (1)

Y2K PROBLEMS - Fenow 20:42:34 6/02/99 (1)
  Re: Y2K PROBLEMS - Haggar 05:31:37 6/03/99 (0)

Super Idiot - Mojoman 19:18:17 6/02/99 (2)
  Re: Super Idiot - BVD'S 19:33:02 6/02/99 (1)
    Re: Idiot - Chuck Wagon 12:37:42 6/03/99 (0)

You think this is funny? I think its stupid, stupid - Stupid 19:18:17 6/02/99 (2)
  Re: You think this is funny? I think its stupid, stupid - Dojoman 19:18:17 6/02/99 (2)
    Re: You think this is funny? I think its stupid, stupid - Mojoman 19:18:17 6/02/99 (2)

Ever join a threaded discussion group
only to get flamed-out...

Why 2K Certified!

...but after Why 2K, flaming
will get really hot.

Y2K Compliant?

Why 2K Certified!

Getting hits used to be one of those
things that you loved to do...

...but these hits aren't so much fun anymore...especially
if you like your teeth.

LOG ON

Y2K Compliant?

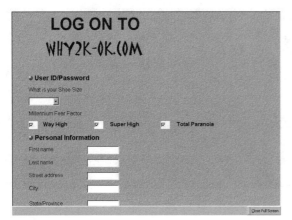

Logging on is as easy as 1-2-3...

Why 2K Certified!

...but after Why 2K it's harder to log off!

CANNED JUNK MAIL

Y2K Compliant?

Maller Daimen:

Are you ready for the Milleniu...

Sex, Sex and More Sex

More Junk Mail

Give me a call.

Karen we should go

How does Brunch sound

Do you get this canned junk when
you open your e-mail everyday...

Why 2K Certified!

...after Why 2K this is what you'll be opening!

ELECTRONIC COMMERCE

Y2K Compliant?

E-Commerce is safe, secure, and ultra cool...

Why 2K Certified!

...but after Why 2K it'll be back to the same old square-wheeled cart... but it will be empty!

SURFING

Y2K Compliant?

Kids from 6 to 60 are surfing from
their PC and a keyboard...

Why 2K Certified!

...but after Why 2K you'll need a
wetsuit and a surfboard!

WEBSITE

Y2K Compliant?

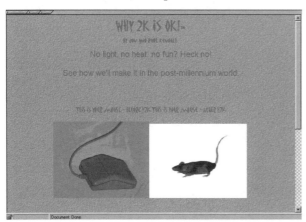

Websites are multiplying at a geometric rate...

Why 2K Certified!

...but after Why 2K the multiplying
will be up to the Black Widow.

Life with Computers

Isn't this what started this thing in the firstplace? It's the Y2K Crisis, stupid.... get ready!

Y2K Compliant?

Installing this application helps you cover
your system before Y2K...

Why 2K Certified!

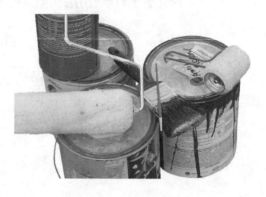

...and after Why 2K this is the only application
you'll be installing!

BATTERY BACKUP SYSTEM

Y2K Compliant?

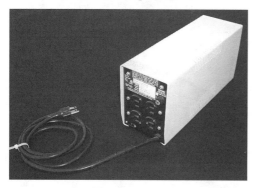

When the power blinks off,
your battery backup kicks in...

Why 2K Certified!

...but after Why 2K,
this is the battery you'll be kicking!

Y2K Compliant?

Why 2K Certified!

111101

Pre-Y2K, computers use thousands of
"ones and zeros" to make up the pattern on the screen...

...after Why 2K, thousands of bites
will make up the pattern on your skin!

CHIPS

Y2K Compliant?

Chips keep getting more and more powerful,
and the price keeps dipping...

Why 2K Certified!

...but after Why 2K, the only things
dipping will be these chips!

HARD DRIVE

Y2K Compliant?

Pre-Y2K hard drives are getting larger, more powerful, and spinning faster...

Why 2K Certified!

...and this post-Why 2K hard drive is getting larger, more powerful, and is spinning faster...and gaining on you!

HARDWARE

Y2K Compliant?

Much of your expensive hardware
will be useless if it is not Y2K compliant...

Why 2K Certified!

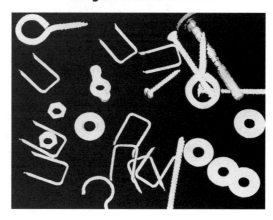

...but this hardware will last until Y3K.

KEYBOARD

Y2K Compliant?

Your keyboard opens the door to cyberspace...

Why 2K Certified!

...after Why 2K, this keyboard will be the only thing that opens the door.

Y2K Compliant?

Your Pre-Y2K laptop is portable, flexible, and stays with you...

Why 2K Certified!

...and after Why 2K your laptop is still portable, flexible, and stays with you!

MACS

Y2K Compliant?

Some macs have problems
digesting PC programs...

Why 2K Certified!

...this could give you post-Why 2K
digestion problems.

Y2K Compliant?

Mainframes are always going to
be with us for heavy lifting applications...

Why 2K Certified!

...but after Why 2K the lifting
will get heavier!

Y2K Compliant?

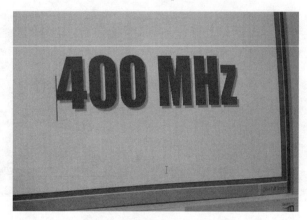

Megahertz denotes the
running ability if your machine...

Why 2K Certified!

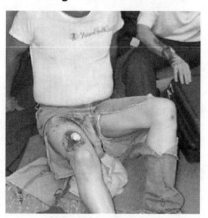

...Why 2K can put a hurt
on your running machine!

MODEM

Y2K Compliant?

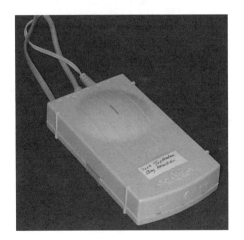

Modems are growing faster and faster...

Why 2K Certified!

...but after Why 2K you'll "modem" fields of growing grass!

MONITOR

Y2K Compliant?

Your monitor is about to...

Why 2K Certified!

...explode with Why 2K!

YOUR MOUSE

Y2K Compliant?

This is your mouse
before Y2K...

Why 2K Certified!

...this is your mouse
after Why 2K... any questions???

OPERATING SYSTEM

Y2K Compliant?

Operating systems are a window that you use to see into cyberspace...

Why 2K Certified!

...but after Why 2K you'll be looking through this window to find your space!

POWER SUPPLY

Y2K Compliant?

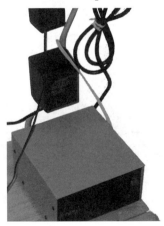

Cords and power supplies get stacked up
as computers evolve...

Why 2K Certified!

...but after Why 2K, these are the only
cords you'll be stacking.

RAM

Y2K Compliant?

If butting up against limited RAM (Random-Access-Memory) gets you nervous before Y2K...

Why 2K Certified!

...imagine how nervous you'll be butting up against this RAM after Why 2K!

SECURE STORAGE

Y2K Compliant?

Gonzo Y2K security analysts make sure that critical data are secure and safe from hackers...

Why 2K Certified!

...but after Why 2K you'll be safe in this package.

Y2K Compliant?

Pre-Y2K software comes in all
shapes and sizes...

Why 2K Certified!

...but so does post-Why 2K software!

SYSTEM FREEZE UP

Y2K Compliant?

A fatal exception (0E: Page Fault) has occurred at 0028:FF01B16
VXD DIGITA(01) + 00001101. Would you like CrashGuard to attempt
recovery from this problem?

Choose OK to have CrashGuard attempt recovery.
Choose Cancel to terminate the current application.

Press <Ctrl+Alt+Del> to restart your computer.
WARNING: You will lose any unsaved information in all applicatio

Press ENTER for OK or ESC to Cancel: OK

Why 2K Certified!

photo by
John Ferguson

Sure enough, your system will freeze up as the ball drops in Times Square...

...and after Why 2K, the freeze could last a long time!

TAPE BACK-UP

Y2K Compliant?

Why 2K Certified!

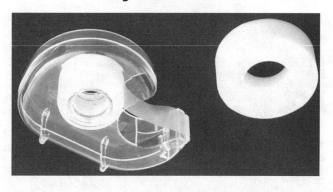

This tape back-up makes sure your pre-Y2K data sticks around...

...and after Why 2K, this tape makes sure your data sticks to the wall!

Life on the Road

Most of us travel these days-on business, on vacation, and driving the kids around. Y2K promises to really bog things down. See how life on the road will be- after Why 2K!

AIRPORT

Y2K Compliant?

Today's airports are crowded, overloaded, and computer-driven...

Why2K Certified!

...but after Why 2K, driving might be a better idea!

AUTOMOBILE

Y2K Compliant?

This baby does zero to sixty in seven seconds...

Why2K Certified!

...and this one does too, if you find the right cliff!

CASH REGISTER

Y2K Compliant?

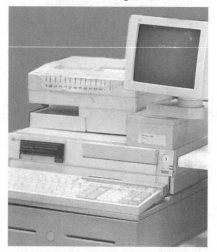

Cash registers like this will stop ringing at Y2K...

Why2K Certified!

...but this one won't!

OVERNIGHT DELIVERY

Y2K Compliant?

Overnight delivery keeps the wheels
of industry moving before Y2K...

Why2K Certified!

...but after, they'll need to reinvent the wheel.

FAST FOOD

Y2K Compliant?

Why2K Certified!

Fast food is computerized today...

...but after Why 2K?

FIRE EQUIPMENT

Y2K Compliant?

This monster needs 15 on-board computers to run...

Why2K Certified!

...but this one needs none!

GAS PUMPS

Y2K Compliant?

Pre-Y2K gas stations use computers to crank out gas...

Why2K Certified!

...but you'll be cranking this after Why 2K!

HOTEL

Y2K Compliant?

Unimagined luxury abounds at pre-Y2K hotels...

Why2K Certified!

...but imagine how this stay will be!

PARKING

Y2K Compliant?

Why2K Certified!

Even parking meters could lock up when we hit Y2K...   ...but you better lock up after Why 2K!

PHONE BOOTH

Y2K Compliant?

Using this high-tech system has coined new phrases...

Why2K Certified!

...but after Why 2K, you'll still need coins!

SUBWAY

Y2K Compliant?

Why2K Certified!

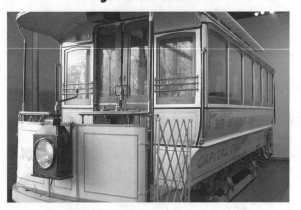

Subways move with computer precision and are neat...

...while post-Why 2K you'll be lucky to find a seat.

TAXICAB

Y2K Compliant?

Taxis now depend on dash-mounted computer screens...

Why2K Certified!

... with this post Why 2K rickshaw, you'll wish you had a screen.

Military

The greatest military power in the world is grappling with Y2K just as you are. See how Post—Why 2K military action might be a bit different...

AIRCRAFT

Y2K Compliant?

Why 2K Certified!

This fighter pushes the envelope of technology...

...while this one needs a push!

MISSILE

Y2K Compliant?

Missile systems are going to match their
targets using computer techology...

Why 2K Certified!

...but this one needs a match.

ROBOT

Y2K Compliant?

Robots have moved to the forefront of military technology...

Why 2K Certified!

...but post-Why 2K robots can
barely count to four!

SATELLITE

Y2K Compliant?

Why 2K Certified!

This satellite needs regular programming...

...but this Satellite won't need it.

SHIP

Y2K Compliant?

This ship sails on technology...

Why 2K Certified!

...while this one sails!

SOLDIER

Y2K Compliant?

Today's soldier is equipped with the
ultimate in information systems...

Why 2K Certified!

...but Post-Why 2K soldiers might
dance to a different drum.

WEAPONS

Y2K Compliant?

Throwing high powered weapons at the enemy
requires rock-solid computer power...

Why 2K Certified!

...but Post-Why 2K weapons will throw rocks!

Office

When we show up for work on Monday, January 3, 2000, things will be different. Really different! See what kind of adjustments we'll make...

CALCULATOR

Y2K Compliant?

Calculators will cease to function...and you'll cuss...

Why 2K Certified!

...but you can always depend on the abacus!

COFFEE

Y2K Compliant?

This java maker needs juice to heat...

Why 2K Certified!

...but this Why 2K pot can heat the juice!

COPIER

Y2K Compliant?

Operating at 50 copies per second,
you'll never need to wait...

Why 2K Certified!

...operating at 5 copies a fortnight,
you'll always need to wait!

CUBES

Y2K Compliant?

These cubes can be a cold, sterile work environment...

Why 2K Certified!

...these cubes are also a cold, sterile environment.

DICTATION RECORDER

Y2K Compliant?

This dictation machine will soon be obsolete...

Why 2K Certified!

...and this one will be hard to feed.

MEETING

Y2K Compliant?

Is this meeting Y2K compliant?

Why 2K Certified!

This meeting is...

MICRORECORDER

Y2K Compliant?

A microrecorder needs to be fed batteries and tapes...

Why 2K Certified!

... a post-why 2K microrecorder needs to be fed seed and water.

SPREADSHEET

Y2K Compliant?

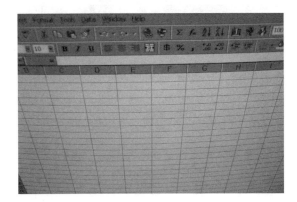

This spreadsheet will get blown away by Y2K...

Why 2K Certified!

...but this spread sheet will get blown dry!

STORAGE

Y2K Compliant?

Random-access storage before Y2K...

Why 2K Certified!

...random-access storage after Why 2K!

WORD PROCESSING

Y2K Compliant?

Don't forget to save your work before the big crash...

Why 2K Certified!

...because afterwards you won't be able to!

Home Life

Imagine...The End of the World As We Know It...

How will we live in a post-millenium world?

Explore home life with us as

we enter the "Why2K Zone!"

Y2K Compliant?

In Case of Emergency, calling for help is as
simple as dialing 911...

Why 2K Certified!

...calling for help gets a whole
lot harder after Why 2K!

BATHROOM

Y2K Compliant?

Before the millenium, these
touches add to your pleasure...

Why 2K Certified!

...but you won't get any pleasure
from touching this!

BOAT

Y2K Compliant?

Boating is a great way to relax before Y2K,
unless you have to bail out...

Why 2K Certified!

...bailing out will be a way
of life in this post-Why 2K yacht!

CLOCK

Y2K Compliant?

This digital clock keeps on ticking
until midnight....

Why 2K Certified!

...but this one keeps on ticking...
if the sun rises on January 1st!

Y2K Compliant?

Modern decor will be out...

Why 2K Certified!

...post-Why 2K decor for mobile living will be in!

OUTDOOR DINING

Y2K Compliant?

Fine dining is one of the simple pleasures of modern life...the conversation rolls on...

Why 2K Certified!

...and after Why 2K, this is what will be rolling!

REFERGERATOR/FREEZER

Y2K Compliant?

Digital ice makers will grind to a halt as the century turns...

Why 2K Certified!

...but this one will grind on.

FURNITURE

Y2K Compliant?

Every modern living room
needs one of these...

Why 2K Certified!

...every post-Why 2K living room
needs one of these.

GROCERY SHOPPING

Y2K Compliant?

The shelves are well stocked before Y2K...

Why 2K Certified!

...after Why 2K there won't be enough for soup stock!

Y2K Compliant?

Why 2K Certified!

Would programming your digital thermostat be a thing of the past after Y2K?

...or "wood" you be programming this thing of the past after Why 2K?

LAMP

Y2K Compliant?

This lamp burns by computer control...

Why 2K Certified!

...after Why 2K this oil lamps burns!

MILK

Y2K Compliant?

These milk containers are lined up before Y2K...

Why 2K Certified!

...and this is a lineup of milk containers after Why 2K!

FOOD PROCESSOR

Y2K Compliant?

This programmable food processor
could quit during your millenium party...

Why 2K Certified!

...but this programmable food processor
won't quit after any party!

OVEN

Y2K Compliant?

Intelligent devices surround us today...

Why 2K Certified!

...but after Why 2K?

CARBON MONOXIDE DETECTOR

Y2K Compliant?

This detector chirps if gas is detected...

Why 2K Certified!

...after Why 2K, this detector **stops** chirping if gas is detected.

POWER

Y2K Compliant?

Every home that depends on this...

Why 2K Certified!

...needs to have this.

SECURITY

Y2K Compliant?

This security system is set up to trigger after an alarm...

Why 2K Certified!

...this security system is set up to trigger before an alarm!

SHOPPING

Y2K Compliant?

Pre-Y2K shopping is a breeze....

Why 2K Certified!

... and so is Why 2K shopping!

SMOKE DETECTOR

Y2K Compliant?

Who knows if this Y2K-compliant
smoke detector will keep sniffing?

Why 2K Certified!

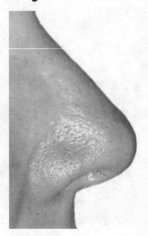

This smoke detector will keep sniffing no matter
who's calendar we follow.

STEREO SYSTEM

Y2K Compliant?

Tune to channels in a stereo
for pre-Y2K sound...

Why 2K Certified!

...tune both to the emergency channel
for post-Why 2K sounds!

VACUUM CLEANERS

Y2K Compliant?

This hypoallergenic HEPA cyclone vac
is the latest technology...

Why 2K Certified!

...this hyper-allergenic Why 2K vac...
you get the idea.

WASHING MACHINES

Y2K Compliant?

Every year, they roll out a new model...

Why 2K Certified!

...but after Why 2K, you'll be rolling out old water.

WATERCRAFT

Y2K Compliant?

Why 2K Certified!

Speeding across the waves before Y2K...

...waving, not speeding after Why 2K!

WELCOME WAGON

Y2K Compliant?

This greets you before Y2K...

Why 2K Certified!

...and this greets you after Why 2K!

Resources

We've done extensive research on "Why 2K is OK" including at least one web search, a trip to the library, and an afternoon at Barnes and Noble at the magazine rack. Here's what we came up with: (Fine Print:Why2K Is OK, of course, makes no representations about any of these sites, as usual in cyberspace, you're on your own, Jack…)

<u>Websites</u>

Check out our website for hats, mugs, t-shirts, etc:
   www.Why2KisOK.com

The Feds Y2K Gateway Site:
   www.itpolicy.gsa.gov/mks/yr2000/y2khome.htm

The Act that Will Save Us All Site:
   www.y2k.gov/

What is Mr. Greenspan up to? Is he stockpiling cash? Check out the Federal Reserve Site:
   www.federalreserve.gov/y2k/

A great Doom and Gloom Site:
   www.garynorth.com

Y2K News/Information Site:
   www.lawpublish.com/y2k-hot.html
   www.y2knews.com/
   y2k.comco.org/

Run this Test on your Computer Site:
   www.cix.co.uk/~harlend/y2k/

Someone Else Thinks This is Funny Site:
   www.doit.state.ct.us/y2k/humor.htm

Even the Big Kahuna has Problems Site:
   www.microsoft.com/technet/year2k/product/product.htm

One Stop Disaster Shopping Site:
   www.year2000goods.com/
   www.y2kchaos.com
   www.y2kequip.com

www.surviveitkits.com

www.y2kwarehouse.com

Now I am Worried…The Red Cross Y2K Site:
www.redcross.org/disaster/safety/y2k.html

"The End of The World As We Know It" Site:
www.teotwawki.org

<u>Y2K - Related Music:</u>

Musicians are working feverishly to come up with Y2K and millenium music. (You can probably find MP3's for these on MP3.com):

Y2K (Wintermute, Notes from Cyber-Space)

Armageddon A-Go-Go (Phoebe Legere, 4 Nurses of the Apocalypse)

Y2K Requiem (Spiral Maze, Beyond the Sands of Time)

<u>Y2K Poetry:</u>

Even Poets have caught the bug:

www.Y2KCulture.com (Solverg Singlton, Y2K hiaku)

Who is the Why2K Millennium Bug Extermination Team?

The Why2K Millennium Bug Extermination Team is a collection of worldwide experts, each one brought in for their specific specialties and detailed knowledge of technology, philosophy, sociology, education, business, management, computers, software, and hardware. This crack team is lead by the brothers Kendall – Jon and Paul.

Jon is the typical Silicon Valley – type technology entrepreneur…only on the wrong coast, without a Stanford education, and without the millions of dollars. He has worked in the technology industry since graduating from college. While still in college, he went to work repairing electronic equipment in a recording studio and tape duplication house. When his tool kit evolved into a wide collection of different sizes and styles of hammers used to hit the sensitive electronic gear ("Oh well Boss, this one is REALLY broken, send it back to the factory"), he realized that he should find

something better to do…or starve to death. At this point, he went to work for technology contractors and learned the craft of technology, systems integration, selling, and management. He found that figuring out what the client needs done and applying the appropriate technology to meet the need actually worked better than throwing technology at the problem hoping that something will work (like the competition seemed to do!). His first startup in 1988, appropriately named Kendall Associates, concentrated on integrating technology into education and healthcare facilities. In 1993, Jon wised up, got some partners (who were smarter than he…not hard…) and formed INTEGREX Systems Corporation. In 1997, INTEGREX was acquired giving Jon the opportunity to do new stuff. Jon's new startup is ideaReserve™ LLC (www.ideareserve.com) an information and publishing firm assisting business, government, and education with seminars, and publications focused on technology, creativity, marketing, and other cool stuff. Jon is also a regular speaker at conferences such as the American Institute of Architects, Society of College and University Planners, and Health Information Management Systems Society on technology, innovation, and the future.

Paul, the typical first-born overachiever, has his undergraduate degree in Environmental Science and Masters in Biological and Agricultural Engineering from Rutgers University in New Brunswick, New Jersey – just the thing for a post-industrial society to rebuild. He received his Juris Doctor degree from the University of Maryland, Baltimore (Yes, another lawyer...). Paul has worked for numerous "Beltway Bandits" (those technology and management firms distributed around the Washington, DC beltway whose sole goal is to relieve the U.S. Government of funds to do "stuff"). His illustrious career has brought him from the intricacies of solar energy ("It's the next big thing! You might need it now that the power's out") to nuclear submarines (no longer necessary), website development, computer programming, and environmental clean up. His background in dealing with the Year 2000 computer problem is rooted in reading newspaper stories and preparing his concrete-lined bomb shelter with soybeans and Pepsi One.

Contributing editor Warren Arbogast was responsible for keeping this project crisp, humorous, to-the-point, and on schedule. Given that the book missed deadline by three months, Warren is confident that no buyers of this book will encounter any Y2K problems until April of the year 2000.

Other members of the team include…well…there are no other members of the team! Just a few guys heavily invested in Millennium Bug Spray futures. Guys who see the future…and the future is…well, not so bad as long as you don't mind BACK BREAKING LABOR, STARVATION, and COLD.

Credits

All photographs were taken by Jon Kendall with his questionably Y2K compliant digital camera.©1999, ideaReserve™, except:

Front cover, page 65 (mouse photos), Pages 19 (reaper), 22, 51 and 64 (melted monitor), 36, 42 and back cover (flaming computer), 48 (surfer), 49 (spiderweb), 68 (ram), 77 (cart), 101 (both meetings), 112 (modern decor), 124 (militia guy), 130 (paddleboat), Images® Copyright 1999 PhotoDisc, Inc.; Page 38, web backbone, courtesy of Dept. of Commerce; Page 45, fallen tree, courtesty of Federal Emergency Management Agency (FEMA), photo by Dave Gately; Page 56, tornado, courtesty of National Oceanographic and Atmospheric Administration; Page 62, mockup of leg injury, courtesy of Federal Emergency Management Agency (FEMA); Page 69, military computer photo, courtesy of US Air Force; Page 71, frozen path, courtesy of Federal Emergency Management Agency (FEMA), photo by John Ferguson; Pages 87 and 94, catapult, unknown; Page 88, F-22, courtesy of

US Air Force, Wright Brother's plane, courtesy of National Park Services; Page 92, advanced ship, sailing ship courtesy of US Navy; Page 93, today's soldier courtesy of US Army; Page 94, Tomahawk missile courtesy US Air Force; Page 107, bunker, courtesy of US Dept. of Defense.

WHY2K IS OK STUFF

Shirts:

**Mouse Tee Shirts
(S, M, L, XL, XXL)**

**Truck Tee Shirts
(S, M, L, XL, XXL)**

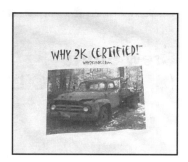

More Shirts:

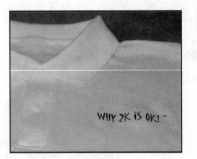

**Polo Shirts
(S, M, L, XL, XXL)**

**Crew Shirts
(S, M, L, XL, XXL)**

Coffee Mugs:

Throw your fellow workers into a Why2K Panic!

Why 2K Calendars and Baseball Hats available, too!

Order On Line: www.Why2KisOK.com